Copyright © 2022 by CHICKEN HOUSE PRESS

All rights reserved. This book or any portion thereof may not be reproduced or used in any manner whatsoever without the express written permission of the author, except for brief excerpts in a book review or journal.

Print ISBN: 978-1-990336-39-3
Contact the publisher for Library and Archives Canada catalogue information.

Temple Grandin photo by Rosalie Winard

chickenhousepress.ca
#awearealldifferentbook

I AM AU-SOME!

AUTISM IS MY SUPERPOWER

FEATURING STUDENTS AND STAFF FROM CHESLEY DISTRICT COMMUNITY SCHOOL

The book will be especially helpful to inform an autistic student's classmates about autism. When other students learn to understand autism, they will be less likely to bully and tease. When I was in elementary school, my third grade teacher explained to the other students that I had a disability that was not visible like a wheelchair. This motivated the other students to be helpful instead of bullying and teasing. *We Are All Different* will motivate classmates to be kind and understanding of an autistic student. They will also learn that their autistic classmate is a unique individual.

Temple Grandin, author
Thinking in Pictures

THROUGH THE LENS OF TEACHERS, SUPPORT WORKERS, AND PEERS

Students with Autism have a special place in my heart. My niece Brooklyn was diagnosed at an early age. She had difficulty communicating her needs and would lash out physically. There were times I was actually scared for my sister. I was in awe of how little support there was for families. Everyone in Brooklynn's life has learned to adapt to her sounds and body language to help understand her. She can still get very angry but is getting a bit better at self-regulating (with assistance). I always wished I understood her better. I wished I knew what she was thinking, feeling, and wanting. She has an amazing sense of humour.

Brooke has a fascination with the police and would often call 911. They would always show up and were so understanding. They just brightened her world. When she started doing that, a lock had to be secured on my sister's phone at all times. Brooklynn is now in her 20's and living somewhat independently in a group home (with others with similar needs), receiving 1:1 support 24/7.

My hope is that this book gives professionals, educators, and families a better understanding of what it is like for families with Autistic children. My hope is that Autistic students will be heard. My hope is that through listening and understanding our students, these students will have a more positive learning experience. My hope is that these students can teach all of us how to be better people.

— MRS. G

Autism is understanding and celebrating the uniqueness and differences that we all have. I have supported those with exceptionalities in a variety of settings and ages for more than 20 years. I have learned alongside those on the Spectrum in both residential and private settings and have spent the last 10 years working in the education sector. Everyone I have worked with has become an integral part of my learning journey. I have learned far more for those whom I have supported than they have ever learned from me. I have been truly honoured and blessed that those I have supported, and their amazing families, trusted me to be a part of their lives in a small way. I have made memories and friendships that will last me a lifetime.

—DEANNA SULKYE, BEHAVIOUR INTERVENTION STUDENT SUPPORT

MEET BAILEY

Bailey is 7 years old and he is in a regular class with withdrawal assistance. He has the support of an Educational Assistant to help him throughout the day. Mrs. Campbell understands his sounds, his flaps, and his facial expressions, and helps the other staff and students around him understand him better too. He is learning how to communicate his needs by pointing to a picture in his communication book and has recently graduated to using an iPad. One of his stimming behaviours is to flap his hands and vocalize loudly when he is excited. Bailey also has a weighted vest, blanket, and a helmet (when needed), which was prescribed by an Occupational Therapist. He is beginning to follow some basic routines, such as putting his boots and shoes where they go, hanging up his coat, and putting away his lunch bag.

Bailey loves water! We have to watch him like a hawk around the salmon tank. If we turn for a second, he's got the lid off and his hands in the water. We often find some toy in there too! It doesn't seem to bother the fish as this is the biggest and healthiest they've ever looked!

Bailey loves to eat pizza, to blow bubbles in his chocolate milk with his straw, and he especially loves to help Mr. Albrecht, our amazing custodian.

  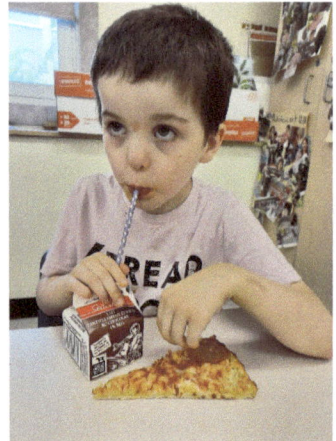 

Bailey is like a ray of sunshine. He brightens my day by greeting me with a snuggle and taking my hand. He extends warmth to others by giving them a high five to say hi.

When he's giggly you can't help but enjoy his infectious laughter and his mischievous grin. His eyes seem to sparkle. This is when he sometimes gets into trouble and says 'oh no,' only to giggle some more.

Bailey loves anything to do with water. This has gotten us into more spills than we can count, even on us!

Bailey is amazing and fun to be with. Bailey has a special place in my heart.

CATHY CAMPBELL (EA)

At a young age Bailey was diagnosed with 17q microdeletion. Bailey is missing his 17th chromosome. After some genetic testing, we discovered his sister Paisley also has the same chromosome missing. After many doctor visits, they told us Bailey will have some development delays.

We had many wonderful, caring people such as Child Infant Development, OT, and Speech therapy come to our house weekly to visit with Bailey. When Bailey was 2 years old, I started noticing that he was flapping his hands, standing only on his tippy toes, and lining trucks up from big to small. This was unusual for him. After some time, Bailey still wasn't meeting his goals for his age. As a concerned parent I started to do more research on the unusual things he would do. After some time I strongly suspected a mild form of Autism. From there, I asked our paediatrician (with letters of support from the Speech Language Pathologist and the Occupational Therapist) if she could confirm my suspicions. I learned that she couldn't actually diagnose but could refer me to someone who could. Thankfully, in a few short visits with a team of doctors observing Bailey, they also came to the conclusion that he had a diagnosis of severe Autism! I will never forget that day; I burst out crying. His doctor asked why I was crying and I couldn't answer because I was crying so hard. "Was it because you knew the diagnosis this whole time?" he asked.

I said yes. I fought for answers for over a year. It was a relief to have a professional confirm what I knew!

From that day forward we have been learning all the aspects of Autism. It's still a learning curve. Bailey is a bright young man who loves water, playing on swings, and playing with his friends at school. He is teaching us every day!

AMANDA WEPPLER, BAILEY'S MOM

MEET GERRET

I was born with autism. While this effects my life, it is not all that I am. I am a human, a boy, a son, a brother, and more. Like anyone else in the world, I am unique. I am not ashamed of being autistic because I am au-some!

Sometimes my autism makes things hard for me. Changes in my routine and new things can be stressful. Sometimes I get really anxious. When I get really angry or sad, my emotions get the best of me. I become so overpowered by them that it often leads to a meltdown. I may say hurtful things so you feel what I feel. I may hurt myself or wreck things I don't really mean to. This is my way of letting it all out. I am still learning the best ways to deal with these situations and how to bring myself back down. It is A LOT to deal with, not just for me but anyone involved. I know this but I can not stop it from happening. The best thing to do is be patient and understanding. Please don't get angry, it will make it worse.

I love to laugh. I enjoy funny things like jokes, movies, books, and shows. When I am interested in something it is my main focus until I move on to the next thing. I love to make ranking lists and talk about things that interest me. My parents joke that I talk all day. I am good at memorizing random facts about things that I have an interest in. I see my memories like pictures in my mind and can replay them in my head like a movie. Sometimes I like to add in my own jokes to make memories funnier. Sometimes I find this relaxing. Life has its ups and downs but I just take it one day at a time.

As a parent of an autistic child, you face many challenges. Talking with other parents is often helpful but remember every child is different and what works for them may not always work for you.

We have experienced many things from toilet training delays, difficulty with social interactions, problems communicating what he wants to say or repeating himself, and anxiety about many things (big or small). While some things improve with age, new things begin.

Our son loved repetitive solo play as a child, then one day he decided he no longer wanted to be alone and would follow me from room to room as he played. He has had many different stims as well, from rocking and humming to chirping and hoping, all of which help him to cope with his day. He tries hard to hold all his stressors in until he is home. While this means dealing with daily meltdowns, this is where he feels safe.

There is also the challenge of balancing other children as well. We try to maintain a set of rules that applies to everyone so no one feels like they are treated unfair. It doesn't always work out but we try.

Even though there are times I want to pull my hair out, there are also so many wonderful times. My son has a great memory, it always amazes me how far back he remembers and the details of that event.

He has an amazing smile, a heart-warming laugh, and a wonderful sense of humour. Given the choice, I would do it all over. I am so proud of the young man he is becoming.

GERRET'S MOM

Meet Jackson

My name is Jackson and I am 11 years old. I am in Grade 6. I am a very cool guy. I love to be around my friends like Gerret - who is also in this book. I like to be around Gerret because he's happy. Sometimes in the classroom it's pretty good and other times it's something totally different. Basically, sometimes we end up doing really cool things, like learning about something new, watching a movie once or twice, and on Tuesday's we even get some supply teachers - which is pretty cool. The other times are awful in every way because I get mad - which is every day, which sucks. Some classmates make fun of me, they ruin my fun. Some classmates know when to stop and appreciate my space. I really like those people because they understand. When I get mad, I'll throw a big fit or get physical. Usually, I'll need to go to the office to cool down. This could take a while but not all the time. Some days you just get over it quickly. Other times it could take a couple of hours.

I wish people would just listen to what I say. I wish people would understand my boundaries and just stop before things got serious.

I like to go outside and use my imagination. I love to make up things in my mind and play. Sometimes though I also like to relax.

I really like video games. They help me calm down, especially if I've had a rough day.

I love to draw. I put my thoughts on paper. I enjoy drawing dinosaurs and any other thing I can think of.

Jackson is my friend. He doesn't like sharing all his personal information, so doing this book is hard for him. Like me, Jackson can get frustrated by things that happen throughout the day. All it takes is one problem to throw off his whole day. Jackson often gets frustrated with the noise level and behaviour of our classmates. Sometimes he yells because he gets so angry. He may even lash out but I don't think he means to. He is just trying to deal with everything that is building up inside him.

Jackson likes to play video games like me. We use to talk about it all the time but not so much anymore. Now we just chat about what's going on.

GERRET

MEET JOE

My name is Joseph Halliday, I'm 14 years old and I have autism, at first I thought this is how people normally act, but in reality,

I am one in a thousand of people who have autism. Autism isn't so bad, some people with autism can do big things, one person with autism got onto a reality show named "Big Brother"!! This proves people like us can do huge things!

Not only do I have Autism, I have ADHD. Sometimes my attention just goes somewhere else. Be patient with me. I will eventually answer you.

I am a computer wizard. I can design my own video games and use them! I also like to draw.

When I grow up I feel like I should make animations or open my own pizza store. People love pizza!!

As a baby Joseph had a hard time self-soothing and would scream a lot. We thought colic maybe, and tried lots of different formulas, but nothing seemed to work other than being held. Once Joseph was a toddler he would jump in his crib for hours and repeated a lot of motions. The word autism and a diagnosis changed our lives. By having a diagnosis it allowed us as a family, and my son as an individual, to understand the many layers involved. My son's quality of life changed and we were able to start to break down the obstacles that made life harder and really pay attention to our environment and how it effected Joseph and our family unit. Our biggest lesson in life is "normal" is different for everyone and we make the best of every day. A lot of things I felt Joseph would or should do never happened, and sometimes we felt disappointed, and then we realized our right is NOT Joseph's right. One of our best techniques is putting our worries on trial. We do the pros and cons to every issue that bothers Joe and break it down on our worry scale. Quite often with our list of pros he is more comfortable or we work on a strategy to help him through it. Every day is unique and special with Joseph and he has touched so many people in a positive way. He makes our life whole.

JOE'S MOM

Joseph does not give his heart and love to just anyone. No matter who you are, you need to earn it through trust and respect. He cares big for all who are in that group. He is still upset about the bees dying. He has drawn plans to open a pizza parlour when he's older. And he talks about when he has a family one day. He is a picky eater and he likes clothes and blankets that are soft and cuddly. He is smart and logical.

GRANDMA IRENE

Being the oldest sister, I have had the joy and privilege of watching Joseph grow and mature through the years. He has taught me so many things that I cherish deeply.

The first is patience: a reminder that everything in life happens at its own pace and we often push for things to happen too quickly. Take time to stop and smell the roses; enjoy the little things that bring you joy; Lego sets aren't built in ten minutes.

Second: the importance of individuality. We can't please everyone. Life's too short for conformity. It's so much more important to be comfortable with who you are.

Third: I will never, ever win at any Mario game. Ever.

Joe continues to amazing me always and I am forever proud of the young man he has become.

CHRISTINE, JOE'S SISTER

Having Joseph in my class has been a pleasure. He's not afraid to embrace his passions and share it with the world. He has an exceptional memory for facts and is always sharing something interesting with us. Also, he is a very accepting student who tries to make everyone feel supported. When faced with a problem, he is always thinking outside the box. Overall, he has been a fantastic addition to our classroom family.

JOE'S TEACHER, JENNA YENSSEN

THOUGHTS FROM JOE'S FRIEND, MARCUS

WHAT IS IT LIKE HAVING A FRIEND WITH AUTISM?

He is nice. We have the same things in common. We like the same things. We like the same video game series. We do chat sometimes on Messenger kids. In the classroom, sometimes he doesn't understand things. He gets frustrated and upset. He'll start to yell. The teacher will tell him to go outside the room and take some breaths. I also try to calm him down. Sometimes it works and sometimes it doesn't. The class is nice to Joe. They are accepting.

IF YOU COULD TELL JOE ONE THING WHAT WOULD IT BE?

That he is the greatest friend I ever had.

Meet Jonah

My name is Jonah Laver. I am in grade 6 and I go to Chesley District Community School. I would like to tell you a little bit about my experience with autism.

When I was younger, I used to get easily frustrated and my EA was the only person who could calm me down. Now I have learned some of my own tools to help. Some of those tools include deep breathing, bouncing a ball, or playing with putty. When loud noises in the classroom bug me, I put on noise cancelling headphones or leave the room. I do not like it when others do not follow the rules, I get terribly upset and must leave the situation. When I was younger, I could not leave the situation, but now I have learned to walk away.

Just because I have autism does not mean I should be excluded from things I just might need a little extra attention than the others or more time to process. I can do everything you can do.

Recently I did a 'Swing Safety' presentation for the classes at CDCS. Most of the classes did learn from the presentations while others maybe didn't pay attention which resulted in students breaking the rules. A couple of months ago I really struggled with presenting in other classes but now I am feeling more confident with myself.

Jonah is an important addition to CDCS, he inspires his peers to be better people by always being honest and caring of others' feelings. Seeing him every day puts a smile on my face and I love getting the chance to chat with him about some of his favourite things, like computers and video games. Getting to know him has been such a lovely experience and I know that he will go on in life to do absolutely incredible things. At the moment his dreams include opening his own restaurant or becoming an office administrator of a school, and I know that if he puts his mind to it he can accomplish these goals with no issues.

EMILY VINCENT (TEACHER)

Meet Malakai

My name is Malakai. I am 12 years old and my superpower is having Autism.

Some things that I would like people to know about me are: sometimes I do certain things over and over again like clearing my throat, tapping my hands, or repeating words or sentences. These are called tics and they help me to calm down if I am scared, happy, or nervous.

Sometimes people that have Autism have other disorders such as ADHD, Anxiety, Speech Disorder, and various others. This makes it difficult to understand which disorder may be causing a meltdown or what the best way to deal with a particular situation would be. For me, my Autism causes me to have a lot of anxiety around loud sounds. I also struggle with wearing specific clothes. These are related to my sensory sensitivities. (My mom tells me that I am the loudest person she knows.) When I am speaking with you, I will take your words very literally. Everything is black and white to me and I have a hard time understanding grey areas. I also experience huge emotions and they can be extreme. I sometimes have a hard time paying attention to detail but sometimes I can pay too much attention to details. I also have a hard time making friends. It is hard for me to understand other people's feelings and emotions and I don't always know what social expectations are required. I also have trouble remembering things and have to be reminded of the same things over and over again. Things like daily chores, rules, and lots of other things too. If you see me taking lots of breaks, it is because I am overstimulated and need to calm my brain down. I usually have so many things going through my mind that it becomes overwhelming and I need to find a way to calm those thoughts down.

My favourite part of having Autism is that I can be really creative, I can be very caring and empathetic, and I can have fun. I just like being me.

WHAT I WOULD WANT PEOPLE TO KNOW ABOUT HAVING A SON ON THE SPECTRUM

I think the biggest thing that I would want people to know about having a child on the spectrum would be that no matter what, I am doing the very best that I can. There are many days that can be absolutely exhausting and frustrating but there are so many other days that are silly and fun. There is never a day that goes by without me learning something new. There is never a dull moment.

Having a child on the spectrum wasn't a choice. At the end of the day, he is my son and I wouldn't change a thing about him (except maybe if he could have slept a little more as a baby). He has taught me more than I could have ever imagined. He has taught me patience, he has taught me how to speak up for the things I believe in, and most importantly to me he has taught me the true meaning of unconditional love. I don't need all the answers, although sometimes I wish I had them, but I can't imagine my life in any other way. He is my hero, my teacher, and the love of my life, and I can't wait to see how many amazing things he will accomplish in his life. I couldn't be more proud of him.

Malakai's school experiences have been mostly positive thus far. Currently he is in Grade 6. He has been attending CDCS since JK.

His first year of school, he struggled with separation anxiety and adjusting to routine changes along with learning how to handle the noise levels of so many children all at once. We chose to only have him attend for half days for his first year so he could adjust to all the changes. We were so fortunate to have such wonderful support from his teachers, EA's, and school support staff at all levels.

Since his first year he has adjusted very well, again with a lot of support, to being at school full days. He has always loved school and participated within his classroom. He has also participated in a select few extra curricular activities with his favourite being cross country.

He had a pretty tight knit group of friends coming up through his elementary grades.

This current year has definitely posed some challenges and we are navigating through some choppy waters. As both he and his friends are getting to their years of puberty and discovering who they are becoming, Malakai has found himself being more anxious and more sensory sensitive than he has been for a long time. This has been a learning curve for both he and I and although it's been a tough few months, we have been offered some wonderful support through his teacher and the school, as well as the school board. For the first time, he has found himself needing headphones to block out some of the excessive loud noises his classroom presents. I know that Malakai is a strong young man and that we will get through this hiccup as a team.

I think overall we have had a wonderful experience with all of the supports we have received and I look forward to seeing what the future will bring to my amazing young man.

SHERI, MALAKAI'S MOM

MEET SOPHIA

WHAT IS IT LIKE HAVING AUTISM?

So its like my brain sometimes has too much stuff in it. It is all cluttered up and it is hard to find the correct one. Like it comes out of the wrong folder. It makes me confused.

WHAT DO YOU WANT THE PEOPLE AROUND YOU TO KNOW?

I would like people to be patient and help when I feel confused.

WHAT ARE YOUR INTERESTS?

Soccer, robot fish, dinosaurs, dragons, science, animals. I love our pets. Oreo (our new cat), Hallie (old cat), Nibbles (my hamster).

WHAT IS IT LIKE HAVING A CHILD WITH AUTISM?

Living with Sophia is a blessing. She is smart, curious, and creative. We also have to remember her differences as well. There has to be patient reminders to correct compulsive behaviours or follow social norms. There can be periods of extreme anxiety about change from routine.

WHAT DO YOU WANT PEOPLE TO KNOW?

I think we should all remember that each of us are fighting own own battles, so always be kind.

Sophia is a grade 4 girl. A day for Sophia runs mostly the same as any other student. Some things maybe be modified but she follows the same routine and day layout as the class. Depending what has gone on in her morning, she may come in with a new fun fact, a bug, or a really cool dinosaur shirt to share with her friends.

Transitions between lessons can come as a challenge for Sophia. Her teacher lays out on her desk what she needs to work on. If you offer her free choice after she's completed her work, she gets very excited. Her favourite free choice would be playing on the computer where she creates her own animations or building her world in Minecraft.

Sophia was recently in the play "Les Trois Petits Cochons." She created her own mask, helped build the houses, and performed her lines on stage in front of other classes. She was incredibly proud of herself and announced she would like to do the play again.

During breaks Sophia will spend her time talking with friends and nibbling lightly on crackers. We encourage her to eat more of her lunch, but she is so excited to enjoy her classmates, she typically talks more than she eats. Once outside, Sophia can be found searching for bugs, hunting snakes, or playing games with her classmates.

Sophia is incredibly smart and creates curious stories, like anyone else though, at times getting to the creating can take her some time. We all get in moods where we just do not want to finish the task at hand, and Sophia is just the same. We work together to find a way to complete the work, but this may involve a break, drawing instead of writing, or switching our space and working at a different table. We work together to make this happen and sometimes we need to get creative to ensure Sophia is supported and successful.

Whether we enjoy Phys Ed outside or inside, Sophia gets involved in the games. If the gym is loud or she is having a hard time concentrating, she will take a break on a scooter board in a small hallway. If we are learning a new game, she prefers to listen to the instructions while in her hallway and watching the game being played first. Once she is ready or asked to join, she leaves the scooter board and plays with her classmates.

Sophia is such a funny girl to work with. I myself feel completely honoured getting to work with her. She challenges me to continue to think about how others learn. What tricks and changes we can make to make learning achievable for everyone in all classroom settings. She shows kindness and caring in so many ways, some loud and some quiet. She is very excited to share in class and sometimes forgets to raise her hand, but her fun facts or what she must share is always curious and creative. Sophias perspective on life is a beautiful view and I love that I get to experience a glimpse of it.

Thank you to the amazing Sophia, you are such a treasure.

JENNA SACHAN

Sophia's drawings L-R: Sophia holding a piece of obsidian rock - she can tell you how it was formed and all of its properties; purple is Sophia's favourite colour; Oreo, the stray cat who adopted her family

www.ingramcontent.com/pod-product-compliance
Lightning Source LLC
Chambersburg PA
CBHW061400090426
42743CB00002B/87